Trauma Recovery
JOURNAL

THIS JOURNAL BELONGS TO:

_____

_____

WELCOME TO YOUR HEALING JOURNAL

This journal is designed to help guide you through your recovery from trauma.

Use the daily prompts when thinking about how your past has impacted your life, and how you will overcome all that you've been through.

This journal is your private space in which to write everything you feel, including your most painful moments and your greatest ones.

I encourage you to read through the journal once you've completed all 90-days of documenting your thoughts and feelings.

Doing so will show you just how far you've come. May it keep you on the road to cleansing your mind, body and spirit.

You can do this.

Day 1:

THE GREATEST CHALLENGE IN YOUR LIFE CURRENTLY IS:

_____

_____

_____

_____

_____

_____

_____

_____

_____

_____

_____

_____

_____

_____

_____

_____

_____

_____

_____

HOW I AM FEELING TODAY

Day 2:

WRITE DOWN 3 WAYS YOU CAN FOCUS ON
DAILY SELF-CARE

_____

_____

_____

_____

_____

_____

_____

_____

_____

_____

_____

_____

_____

_____

_____

_____

_____

_____

_____

_____

_____

_____

HOW I AM FEELING TODAY

Day 3:

DESCRIBE YOUR SAFE SPACE:

_____
_____
_____
_____
_____
_____
_____
_____
_____
_____
_____
_____
_____
_____
_____
_____
_____
_____
_____
_____
_____
_____
_____
_____

HOW I AM FEELING TODAY

Day 4:

WRITE ABOUT YOUR TAKE ON FORGIVENESS:

_____

_____

_____

_____

_____

_____

_____

_____

_____

_____

_____

_____

_____

_____

_____

_____

_____

_____

_____

_____

_____

_____

HOW I AM FEELING TODAY

Day 5:

WRITE A LETTER TO YOUR YOUNGER SELF:

_____

_____

_____

_____

_____

_____

_____

_____

_____

_____

_____

_____

_____

_____

_____

_____

_____

_____

_____

_____

_____

HOW I AM FEELING TODAY

Day 6:

WRITE A LETTER TO YOUR FUTURE SELF:

_____
_____
_____
_____
_____
_____
_____
_____
_____
_____
_____
_____
_____
_____
_____
_____
_____
_____
_____
_____
_____
_____
_____
_____
_____
_____
_____

HOW I AM FEELING TODAY

Day 7:

WRITE ABOUT A TRAUMA RESPONSE YOU ARE
WORKING ON:

_____
_____
_____
_____
_____
_____
_____
_____
_____
_____
_____
_____
_____
_____
_____
_____
_____
_____
_____
_____

HOW I AM FEELING TODAY

Day 8:

WRITE ABOUT A DIFFICULT SITUATION
THAT YOU'VE OVERCOME:

_____
_____
_____
_____
_____
_____
_____
_____
_____
_____
_____
_____
_____
_____
_____
_____
_____
_____
_____
_____
_____
_____

HOW I AM FEELING TODAY

Day 9:

LIST 5 THINGS THAT BRING YOU JOY:

_____

_____

_____

_____

_____

_____

_____

_____

_____

_____

_____

_____

_____

_____

_____

_____

_____

_____

_____

_____

_____

_____

HOW I AM FEELING TODAY

Day 10:

IF YOU COULD TELL YOUR STORY TO ONLY
ONE PERSON WITHIN JUST 10-MINUTES,
WHAT WOULD YOU SAY?:

_____

_____

_____

_____

_____

_____

_____

_____

_____

_____

_____

_____

_____

_____

_____

_____

_____

_____

_____

_____

_____

_____

HOW I AM FEELING TODAY

Day 11:

WHO BELIEVED YOU? DESCRIBE THEM:

_____
_____
_____
_____
_____
_____
_____
_____
_____
_____
_____
_____
_____
_____
_____
_____
_____
_____
_____
_____
_____
_____
_____
_____

HOW I AM FEELING TODAY

Day 12:

DO YOU HAVE DIFFICULTY SETTING BOUNDARIES? EXPLAIN BELOW:

_____
_____
_____
_____
_____
_____
_____
_____
_____
_____
_____
_____
_____
_____
_____
_____
_____
_____
_____
_____
_____
_____

HOW I AM FEELING TODAY

Day 13:

DO YOU HAVE A HISTORY OF FEELING
HELPLESS? DESCRIBE THAT BELOW:

_____

_____

_____

_____

_____

_____

_____

_____

_____

_____

_____

_____

_____

_____

_____

_____

_____

_____

_____

HOW I AM FEELING TODAY

Day 14:

HAVE YOU EVER BEEN IN DENIAL BECAUSE
YOU WANTED TO SEE THE BEST IN PEOPLE?
WRITE DOWN YOUR THOUGHTS BELOW:

_____

_____

_____

_____

_____

_____

_____

_____

_____

_____

_____

_____

_____

_____

_____

_____

_____

_____

_____

_____

HOW I AM FEELING TODAY

Day 15:

DESCRIBE YOUR TOP TRIGGERS:

_____
_____
_____
_____
_____
_____
_____
_____
_____
_____
_____
_____
_____
_____
_____
_____
_____
_____
_____
_____
_____

HOW I AM FEELING TODAY

Day 16:

DESCRIBE YOUR TOP SELF-SOOTHING
TECHNIQUES BELOW:

_____
_____
_____
_____
_____
_____
_____
_____
_____
_____
_____
_____
_____
_____
_____
_____
_____
_____
_____
_____
_____
_____

HOW I AM FEELING TODAY

Day 17:

LIST 3 POSITIVE QUALITIES OR STRENGTHS THAT YOU VALUE IN YOURSELF:

_____
_____
_____
_____
_____
_____
_____
_____
_____
_____
_____
_____
_____
_____
_____
_____
_____
_____
_____
_____
_____

HOW I AM FEELING TODAY

Day 18:

LIST 5 ROLES OR LABELS THAT YOU
BELIEVE DEFINE YOU:

_____

_____

_____

_____

_____

_____

_____

_____

_____

_____

_____

_____

_____

_____

_____

_____

_____

_____

_____

_____

_____

_____

HOW I AM FEELING TODAY

Day 19:

WRITE A LETTER TO YOUR LOVED ONES.
WHAT IS IN YOUR HEART?

_____

_____

_____

_____

_____

_____

_____

_____

_____

_____

_____

_____

_____

_____

_____

_____

_____

_____

_____

_____

HOW I AM FEELING TODAY

Day 20:

THINK OF ONE THING YOU NEED RIGHT
NOW. WRITE OUT HOW YOU MAY
COMMUNICATE THIS TO OTHERS.

_____
_____
_____
_____
_____
_____
_____
_____
_____
_____
_____
_____
_____
_____
_____
_____
_____
_____
_____
_____
_____
_____
_____
_____
_____

HOW I AM FEELING TODAY

Day 21:

DESCRIBE HOW THIS TRAUMA HAS INFLUENCED ASPECTS OF YOUR LIFE:

_____
_____
_____
_____
_____
_____
_____
_____
_____
_____
_____
_____
_____
_____
_____
_____
_____
_____
_____
_____
_____
_____

HOW I AM FEELING TODAY

Day 22:

IN WHAT WAYS HAS THIS TRAUMA MADE YOU MORE VULNERABLE?

_____
_____
_____
_____
_____
_____
_____
_____
_____
_____
_____
_____
_____
_____
_____
_____
_____
_____
_____
_____
_____
_____
_____
_____

HOW I AM FEELING TODAY

Day 23:

IN WHAT WAYS HAS THIS TRAUMA MADE YOU LESS VULNERABLE?

_____
_____
_____
_____
_____
_____
_____
_____
_____
_____
_____
_____
_____
_____
_____
_____
_____
_____
_____
_____
_____
_____

HOW I AM FEELING TODAY

Day 24:

WRITE ABOUT THE EVENT IN THIRD PERSON
AS THOUGH IT HAPPENED TO SOMEONE
ELSE:

_____

_____

_____

_____

_____

_____

_____

_____

_____

_____

_____

_____

_____

_____

_____

_____

_____

_____

_____

_____

_____

_____

_____

_____

_____

_____

HOW I AM FEELING TODAY

Day 25:

START TODAY'S ENTRY WITH "IF THIS HAD NEVER HAPPENED...":

_____
_____
_____
_____
_____
_____
_____
_____
_____
_____
_____
_____
_____
_____
_____
_____
_____
_____
_____
_____
_____
_____

HOW I AM FEELING TODAY

Day 26:

DESCRIBE WHAT MAKES YOU THE ANGRIEST AND HOW YOU REACT TO THAT ANGER:

_____

_____

_____

_____

_____

_____

_____

_____

_____

_____

_____

_____

_____

_____

_____

_____

_____

_____

_____

_____

_____

_____

HOW I AM FEELING TODAY

Day 27:

WRITE DOWN A POSITIVE AFFIRMATION OR
A QUOTE THAT INSPIRES YOU:

_____

_____

_____

_____

_____

_____

_____

_____

_____

_____

_____

_____

_____

_____

_____

_____

_____

_____

_____

_____

_____

HOW I AM FEELING TODAY

Day 28:

WRITE ABOUT A NEGATIVE COGNITION YOU HOLD THAT YOU KNOW ISN'T TRUE:

_____
_____
_____
_____
_____
_____
_____
_____
_____
_____
_____
_____
_____
_____
_____
_____
_____
_____
_____
_____
_____
_____
_____
_____

HOW I AM FEELING TODAY

Day 29:

WHAT HAUNTS YOU THE MOST? EXPLORE YOUR STORY BELOW:

_____
_____
_____
_____
_____
_____
_____
_____
_____
_____
_____
_____
_____
_____
_____
_____
_____
_____
_____
_____
_____
_____

HOW I AM FEELING TODAY

Day 30:

I HAVE NEVER TALKED ABOUT THIS...

_____
_____
_____
_____
_____
_____
_____
_____
_____
_____
_____
_____
_____
_____
_____
_____
_____
_____
_____
_____
_____
_____

HOW I AM FEELING TODAY

Day 31:

THE HARDEST LIE I EVER TOLD WAS...

_____
_____
_____
_____
_____
_____
_____
_____
_____
_____
_____
_____
_____
_____
_____
_____
_____
_____
_____
_____
_____

HOW I AM FEELING TODAY

Day 32:

THE WAY IT REALLY HAPPENED...

_____
_____
_____
_____
_____
_____
_____
_____
_____
_____
_____
_____
_____
_____
_____
_____
_____
_____
_____
_____
_____
_____
_____

HOW I AM FEELING TODAY

Day 33:

THE STORY HIDDEN IN THE BACK OF MY MIND BEGINS LIKE THIS...

_____

_____

_____

_____

_____

_____

_____

_____

_____

_____

_____

_____

_____

_____

_____

_____

_____

_____

_____

_____

HOW I AM FEELING TODAY

Day 34:

THE THING THAT WEIGHS HEAVIEST ON MY HEART IS...

_____
_____
_____
_____
_____
_____
_____
_____
_____
_____
_____
_____
_____
_____
_____
_____
_____
_____
_____
_____
_____
_____
_____

HOW I AM FEELING TODAY

Day 35:

DO YOU THINK OF YOURSELF AS A VICTIM? A SURVIVOR? EXPLAIN BELOW:

_____
_____
_____
_____
_____
_____
_____
_____
_____
_____
_____
_____
_____
_____
_____
_____
_____
_____
_____

HOW I AM FEELING TODAY

Day 36:

WHAT DO YOU FEEL IS HOLDING YOU BACK FROM MOVING PAST THE TRAUMA?

_____

_____

_____

_____

_____

_____

_____

_____

_____

_____

_____

_____

_____

_____

_____

_____

_____

_____

_____

_____

_____

_____

_____

HOW I AM FEELING TODAY

Day 37:

LIST 3 THINGS YOU CAN DO TO START MOVING FORWARD:

_____
_____
_____
_____
_____
_____
_____
_____
_____
_____
_____
_____
_____
_____
_____
_____
_____
_____
_____
_____
_____
_____
_____

HOW I AM FEELING TODAY

Day 38:

THINK ABOUT ONE TIME WHERE YOU FELT
SOMEONE LET YOU DOWN. DESCRIBE HOW
YOU FELT IN THAT MOMENT:

_____

_____

_____

_____

_____

_____

_____

_____

_____

_____

_____

_____

_____

_____

_____

_____

_____

_____

_____

_____

_____

HOW I AM FEELING TODAY

Day 39:

HOW OFTEN DO YOU FIND YOURSELF OVER-THINKING? WHAT DO YOU THINK ABOUT MOST?

_____
_____
_____
_____
_____
_____
_____
_____
_____
_____
_____
_____
_____
_____
_____
_____
_____
_____

HOW I AM FEELING TODAY

Day 40:

WHAT ARE YOUR CORE VALUES? WHAT IS MOST IMPORTANT TO YOU?

_____
_____
_____
_____
_____
_____
_____
_____
_____
_____
_____
_____
_____
_____
_____
_____
_____
_____
_____
_____
_____
_____
_____
_____
_____

HOW I AM FEELING TODAY

Day 41:

WHEN ARE YOU HARDEST ON YOURSELF?

_____
_____
_____
_____
_____
_____
_____
_____
_____
_____
_____
_____
_____
_____
_____
_____
_____
_____
_____
_____
_____
_____

HOW I AM FEELING TODAY

Day 42:

WHAT NEGATIVE EMOTIONS ARE YOU COMFORTABLE SITTING WITH? DESCRIBE:

_____
_____
_____
_____
_____
_____
_____
_____
_____
_____
_____
_____
_____
_____
_____
_____
_____
_____
_____
_____
_____
_____
_____

HOW I AM FEELING TODAY

Day 43:

HOW DID YOU PROCESS EMOTIONS AS A CHILD?

_____
_____
_____
_____
_____
_____
_____
_____
_____
_____
_____
_____
_____
_____
_____
_____
_____
_____
_____
_____
_____

HOW I AM FEELING TODAY

Day 44:

HOW DO YOU ENFORCE BOUNDARIES?

_____
_____
_____
_____
_____
_____
_____
_____
_____
_____
_____
_____
_____
_____
_____
_____
_____
_____
_____
_____
_____
_____
_____
_____
_____

HOW I AM FEELING TODAY

Day 45:

HOW DO YOU CARRY THE WEIGHT OF YOUR
PAST TRAUMA? HOW HAS IT AFFECTED YOU?

_____
_____
_____
_____
_____
_____
_____
_____
_____
_____
_____
_____
_____
_____
_____
_____
_____
_____
_____
_____

HOW I AM FEELING TODAY

Day 46:

DID YOU HAVE ANY HEROES GROWING UP? WHO DID YOU LOOK UP TO AND WHY?

_____
_____
_____
_____
_____
_____
_____
_____
_____
_____
_____
_____
_____
_____
_____
_____
_____
_____
_____
_____
_____
_____
_____

HOW I AM FEELING TODAY

Day 47:

HOW DO YOU DEAL WITH NEGATIVE EMOTIONS AT THIS POINT IN YOUR LIFE?

_____
_____
_____
_____
_____
_____
_____
_____
_____
_____
_____
_____
_____
_____
_____
_____
_____
_____
_____
_____

HOW I AM FEELING TODAY

Day 48:

WHAT'S THE ONE THING YOU WISH OTHERS KNEW ABOUT YOUR AUTHENTIC SELF?

_____

_____

_____

_____

_____

_____

_____

_____

_____

_____

_____

_____

_____

_____

_____

_____

_____

_____

_____

_____

_____

_____

HOW I AM FEELING TODAY

Day 49:

WRITE DOWN WHAT YOUR LIFE WILL LOOK LIKE WHEN YOU'VE OVERCOME THIS TRAUMA:

_____

_____

_____

_____

_____

_____

_____

_____

_____

_____

_____

_____

_____

_____

_____

_____

_____

_____

_____

_____

_____

HOW I AM FEELING TODAY

Day 50:

HOW DO YOU FEEL ABOUT CONFRONTATION? DESCRIBE YOUR REACTIONS/FEELINGS:

_____
_____
_____
_____
_____
_____
_____
_____
_____
_____
_____
_____
_____
_____
_____
_____
_____
_____
_____
_____
_____
_____
_____
_____

HOW I AM FEELING TODAY

Day 51:

DESCRIBE THE WAYS YOU SELF-SOOTHE:

_____

_____

_____

_____

_____

_____

_____

_____

_____

_____

_____

_____

_____

_____

_____

_____

_____

_____

_____

_____

HOW I AM FEELING TODAY

Day 52:

HOW COULD YOU USE YOUR PAIN TO CHANGE SITUATIONS OR HELP SOMEONE ELSE?

_____
_____
_____
_____
_____
_____
_____
_____
_____
_____
_____
_____
_____
_____
_____
_____
_____
_____
_____
_____
_____
_____
_____

HOW I AM FEELING TODAY

Day 53:

WHAT PREVENTS YOU THE MOST FROM LIVING LIFE ON YOUR OWN TERMS?

_____

_____

_____

_____

_____

_____

_____

_____

_____

_____

_____

_____

_____

_____

_____

_____

_____

_____

_____

_____

_____

_____

_____

HOW I AM FEELING TODAY

Day 54:

WHAT ARE YOUR UNMET NEEDS THAT YOU
DON'T BELIEVE YOU CAN FULFILL YOURSELF?

_____
_____
_____
_____
_____
_____
_____
_____
_____
_____
_____
_____
_____
_____
_____
_____
_____
_____
_____
_____

HOW I AM FEELING TODAY

Day 55:

WHAT THOUGHTS HAVE TROUBLED YOU THE MOST TODAY? WRITE THEM BELOW:

_____

_____

_____

_____

_____

_____

_____

_____

_____

_____

_____

_____

_____

_____

_____

_____

_____

_____

_____

HOW I AM FEELING TODAY

Day 56:

WRITE A NOTE FROM YOUR WISE AND
AUTHENTIC SELF TO THE SIDE OF YOU
THAT CAN'T ALWAYS SEE REASON:

_____

_____

_____

_____

_____

_____

_____

_____

_____

_____

_____

_____

_____

_____

_____

_____

_____

_____

_____

_____

_____

_____

_____

HOW I AM FEELING TODAY

Day 57:

WRITE A LIST OF PEOPLE THAT YOU NEED TO FORGIVE:

_____

_____

_____

_____

_____

_____

_____

_____

_____

_____

_____

_____

_____

_____

_____

_____

_____

_____

_____

_____

_____

HOW I AM FEELING TODAY

Day 58:

WRITE A LETTER TO ONE OF THE PEOPLE
FROM DAY 57:

_____
_____
_____
_____
_____
_____
_____
_____
_____
_____
_____
_____
_____
_____
_____
_____
_____
_____
_____
_____
_____
_____
_____

HOW I AM FEELING TODAY

Day 59:

HOW DO YOU DRAW STRENGTH FROM LOVED ONE? DESCRIBE THIS BELOW:

_____

_____

_____

_____

_____

_____

_____

_____

_____

_____

_____

_____

_____

_____

_____

_____

_____

_____

_____

_____

_____

HOW I AM FEELING TODAY

Day 60:

WHO DO YOU TRUST MOST? WHY DO YOU FEEL YOU CAN TRUST THEM?

_____

_____

_____

_____

_____

_____

_____

_____

_____

_____

_____

_____

_____

_____

_____

_____

_____

_____

_____

_____

_____

_____

_____

HOW I AM FEELING TODAY

Day 61:

WHAT DO YOU VALUE MOST IN YOUR CURRENT FRIENDSHIPS?

_____
_____
_____
_____
_____
_____
_____
_____
_____
_____
_____
_____
_____
_____
_____
_____
_____
_____
_____

HOW I AM FEELING TODAY

Day 62:

HOW DO YOU SHOW COMPASSION TO OTHERS?

HOW I AM FEELING TODAY

Day 63:

WHAT BOUNDARIES DO YOU FEEL YOU NEED TO WORK ON SETTING?

_____
_____
_____
_____
_____
_____
_____
_____
_____
_____
_____
_____
_____
_____
_____
_____
_____
_____
_____

HOW I AM FEELING TODAY

Day 64:

NAME 2 WAYS YOU FEEL YOU CAN BETTER
SUPPORT AND APPRECIATE YOURSELF:

_____
_____
_____
_____
_____
_____
_____
_____
_____
_____
_____
_____
_____
_____
_____
_____
_____
_____
_____
_____
_____
_____

HOW I AM FEELING TODAY

Day 65:

WHAT FULFILLS YOU THE MOST IN YOUR LIFE AT THIS MOMENT IN TIME?

_____
_____
_____
_____
_____
_____
_____
_____
_____
_____
_____
_____
_____
_____
_____
_____
_____
_____
_____
_____

HOW I AM FEELING TODAY

Day 66:

WHICH EMOTIONS DO YOU FIND HARDEST TO ACCEPT? (GUILT, ANGER, ETC.)

_____

_____

_____

_____

_____

_____

_____

_____

_____

_____

_____

_____

_____

_____

_____

_____

_____

_____

_____

_____

_____

_____

HOW I AM FEELING TODAY

Day 67:

WHAT DO YOU FEAR THE MOST?

_____

_____

_____

_____

_____

_____

_____

_____

_____

_____

_____

_____

_____

_____

_____

_____

_____

_____

_____

HOW I AM FEELING TODAY

Day 68:

HOW DO YOU SHOW YOURSELF KINDNESS?

HOW I AM FEELING TODAY

Day 69:

WHAT PLACE MAKES YOU FEEL MOST AT PEACE?

_____
_____
_____
_____
_____
_____
_____
_____
_____
_____
_____
_____
_____
_____
_____
_____
_____
_____
_____
_____

HOW I AM FEELING TODAY

Day 70:

WHEN DO YOU FEEL MOST POWERFUL?

_____
_____
_____
_____
_____
_____
_____
_____
_____
_____
_____
_____
_____
_____
_____
_____
_____
_____
_____
_____
_____

HOW I AM FEELING TODAY

Day 71:

WHAT FEELINGS DO YOU EXPERIENCE WHEN YOU RELIVE THE TRAUMA?

_____

_____

_____

_____

_____

_____

_____

_____

_____

_____

_____

_____

_____

_____

_____

_____

_____

_____

_____

_____

_____

HOW I AM FEELING TODAY

Day 72:

WHAT KIND OF LIFE WOULD MAKE YOU FEEL SAFE & FULFILLED?

_____

_____

_____

_____

_____

_____

_____

_____

_____

_____

_____

_____

_____

_____

_____

_____

_____

_____

_____

_____

_____

_____

HOW I AM FEELING TODAY

Day 73:

IDENTIFY TOXIC SOURCES/PEOPLE IN YOUR
LIFE BELOW:

_____

_____

_____

_____

_____

_____

_____

_____

_____

_____

_____

_____

_____

_____

_____

_____

_____

_____

_____

HOW I AM FEELING TODAY

Day 74:

WHEN WAS THE LAST TIME YOU CRIED? DESCRIBE THE SITUATION BELOW:

_____

_____

_____

_____

_____

_____

_____

_____

_____

_____

_____

_____

_____

_____

_____

_____

_____

_____

_____

_____

_____

_____

_____

_____

HOW I AM FEELING TODAY

Day 75:

DESCRIBE YOUR SUPPORT TEAM OR SYSTEM
IN THE SPACE BELOW:

_____
_____
_____
_____
_____
_____
_____
_____
_____
_____
_____
_____
_____
_____
_____
_____
_____
_____
_____
_____
_____

HOW I AM FEELING TODAY

Day 76:

DEEP DOWN, WHAT DO YOU FEEL YOUR PURPOSE IS IN LIFE?

HOW I AM FEELING TODAY

Day 77:

WRITE DOWN 3 SMALL THINGS YOU CAN DO
THAT WILL HAVE A LONG-TERM POSITIVE
IMPACT ON YOUR LIFE:

_____
_____
_____
_____
_____
_____
_____
_____
_____
_____
_____
_____
_____
_____
_____
_____
_____
_____
_____
_____
_____
_____

HOW I AM FEELING TODAY

Day 78:

WHAT IS YOUR DEFINITION OF HAPPINESS?

_____
_____
_____
_____
_____
_____
_____
_____
_____
_____
_____
_____
_____
_____
_____
_____
_____
_____
_____
_____
_____
_____
_____

HOW I AM FEELING TODAY

Day 79:

WHAT IS YOUR MOST CHERISHED RECENT MEMORY AND WHY?

_____

_____

_____

_____

_____

_____

_____

_____

_____

_____

_____

_____

_____

_____

_____

_____

_____

_____

_____

_____

_____

_____

_____

_____

_____

HOW I AM FEELING TODAY

Day 80:

DESCRIBE A PAST EXPERIENCE WHERE YOU
OVERCAME PAIN, FEAR OR FAILURE:

_____
_____
_____
_____
_____
_____
_____
_____
_____
_____
_____
_____
_____
_____
_____
_____
_____
_____
_____
_____
_____
_____
_____

HOW I AM FEELING TODAY

Day 81:

WRITE DOWN A TIME WHEN SOMEONE ELSE HELPED YOU DEAL WITH YOUR PAIN:

_____
_____
_____
_____
_____
_____
_____
_____
_____
_____
_____
_____
_____
_____
_____
_____
_____
_____
_____
_____

HOW I AM FEELING TODAY

Day 82:

IF YOU COULD SOLVE ONE PROBLEM IN YOUR LIFE, WHAT WOULD IT BE?

_____
_____
_____
_____
_____
_____
_____
_____
_____
_____
_____
_____
_____
_____
_____
_____
_____
_____
_____
_____
_____
_____

HOW I AM FEELING TODAY

Day 83:

WHAT WOULD THE 5-YEAR OLD YOU THINK
ABOUT WHERE YOU ARE TODAY?

_____

_____

_____

_____

_____

_____

_____

_____

_____

_____

_____

_____

_____

_____

_____

_____

_____

_____

_____

_____

HOW I AM FEELING TODAY

Day 84:

WHEN WAS THE LAST TIME YOU SAID "NO'
TO SOMETHING AND WISHED YOU HAD SAID
YES. DESCRIBE THE SITUATION BELOW:

_____

_____

_____

_____

_____

_____

_____

_____

_____

_____

_____

_____

_____

_____

_____

_____

_____

_____

_____

_____

_____

_____

HOW I AM FEELING TODAY

Day 85:

WHERE IN YOUR LIFE DO YOU FEEL DISORGANIZED? HOW YOU CAN IMPROVE?

_____

_____

_____

_____

_____

_____

_____

_____

_____

_____

_____

_____

_____

_____

_____

_____

_____

_____

HOW I AM FEELING TODAY

Day 86:

WHEN WAS THE LAST TIME YOU SURPRISED
YOURSELF? DESCRIBE IT BELOW:

_____

_____

_____

_____

_____

_____

_____

_____

_____

_____

_____

_____

_____

_____

_____

_____

_____

_____

_____

_____

_____

_____

_____

HOW I AM FEELING TODAY

Day 87:

WHAT IS YOUR DEFINITION OF SUCCESS?

_____

_____

_____

_____

_____

_____

_____

_____

_____

_____

_____

_____

_____

_____

_____

_____

_____

_____

HOW I AM FEELING TODAY

Day 88:

WRITE DOWN 5 WAYS YOU CAN REDUCE
STRESS AND AXIETY FROM YOUR LIFE:

_____
_____
_____
_____
_____
_____
_____
_____
_____
_____
_____
_____
_____
_____
_____
_____
_____
_____
_____
_____
_____
_____
_____

HOW I AM FEELING TODAY

Day 89:

WRITE DOWN 2 THINGS YOU CAN DO TO
TRAIN YOUR AUTHENTIC SELF-EXPRESSION:

_____

_____

_____

_____

_____

_____

_____

_____

_____

_____

_____

_____

_____

_____

_____

_____

_____

_____

_____

_____

_____

HOW I AM FEELING TODAY

Day 90:

YOU'VE MADE IT TO DAY 90! ON THIS
FINAL PAGE, WRITE DOWN WHO YOU ARE
AND WHO YOU ARE MEANT TO BE:

_____

_____

_____

_____

_____

_____

_____

_____

_____

_____

_____

_____

_____

_____

_____

_____

_____

_____

_____

_____

_____

_____

HOW I AM FEELING TODAY

Notes:

Notes:

Notes:

_____

_____

_____

_____

_____

_____

_____

_____

_____

_____

_____

_____

_____

_____

_____

_____

_____

_____

_____

_____

Notes:

_____

_____

_____

_____

_____

_____

_____

_____

_____

_____

_____

_____

_____

_____

_____

_____

_____

_____

Notes:

_____
_____
_____
_____
_____
_____
_____
_____
_____
_____
_____
_____
_____
_____
_____
_____
_____
_____
_____

Notes:

Notes:

_____

_____

_____

_____

_____

_____

_____

_____

_____

_____

_____

_____

_____

_____

_____

_____

_____

_____

Made in the USA
Las Vegas, NV
26 November 2024

12689318R00056